AF363002

Your Heart, My Home

A Collection of Soulful Poems

Jyoti Juneja

BookLeaf Publishing

India | USA | UK

Copyright © Jyoti Juneja
All Rights Reserved.

This book has been self-published with all reasonable efforts taken to make the material error-free by the author. No part of this book shall be used, reproduced in any manner whatsoever without written permission from the author, except in the case of brief quotations embodied in critical articles and reviews.

The Author of this book is solely responsible and liable for its content including but not limited to the views, representations, descriptions, statements, information, opinions, and references ["Content"]. The Content of this book shall not constitute or be construed or deemed to reflect the opinion or expression of the Publisher or Editor. Neither the Publisher nor Editor endorse or approve the Content of this book or guarantee the reliability, accuracy, or completeness of the Content published herein and do not make any representations or warranties of any kind, express or implied, including but not limited to the implied warranties of merchantability, fitness for a particular purpose.
The Publisher and Editor shall not be liable whatsoever...

Made with ❤ on the BookLeaf Publishing Platform
www.bookleafpub.in
www.bookleafpub.com

Dedication

To the God residing in the hearts of every living being.

To the unique souls, dreamers, weirdos, the black sheep,
the rejects, the eccentrics, the loners, and the lost souls
in the journey of self-discovery.

Om Tat Sat

Preface

To My Dearest Readers,

Life is often a mystery to all of us. Sometimes we don't understand where we are heading to, and everything seems directionless and purposeless. Sometimes we find ourselves lost amidst the hustle bustle of life, but the worst part is not even realizing that we are lost. So, if you are struggling to find your way out, then consider yourself lucky. If you are seeking something that sparks your soul, chasing your dreams or doing what makes you feel alive, then no matter where it leads to. You are on the right path, my friend.

Struggle is inevitable. The journey to success is usually marked by twists and turns, but worth enduring all the challenges turning you into a polished diamond that shines the brightest. Also, a life without struggles makes no account in history, and it's often a plot with the twists and turns that marks a marvelous story.

We are the writers of our own story, the story of life. Indeed, there are certain things that are beyond our control in our life. But, believe in yourself and your dreams. You have been given those dreams for a reason. No matter how impossible it might seem, everything is possible for the spirit that refuses to give up. Always listen to those whispers of the soul in the depths of your heart, where your dreams dwell.

The title "Your Heart, My Home" justifies the poetic journey of a dreamer, a lover, and a misfit, whose struggles against the odds embarks on the journey of self-belief, self-love and self-discovery. You might encounter a million critics on the path to soul purpose. Stick to your inner voice, the voice of your soul, regardless of what others feel or think. History belongs to those who dare to dream and pave their own path of destiny, that the mainstream is fearful of doing. For the cost of not following dreams is a lifeless life, mere surviving and not getting anywhere, let your hearts be a home to your dreams, faith and self-belief. Trying hard and failing is much better than the regrets at the deathbed. Live life to the fullest, be grateful and cherish every moment of your life.

Let your hearts be the home to your dreams.
Let your hard work pave the road to success.
Let yourself enjoy the journey of life while you
can.

With best regards,
Jyoti Juneja

Acknowledgements

I'd like to express my heartfelt gratitude towards the Almighty Lord, my guardian angel, who navigated me through the ups and downs of my life, who created this vast, enchanting, mysterious Universe that intrigues and inspires me, and who gave me this beautiful life.

I am deeply grateful to my family and my admirers for their unwavering encouragement. Their love and support have always been my guiding light.

I express my gratitude to the muses — the moments of beauty, pain, and wonder that have sparked the verses within these pages.

Thank you from the bottom of my heart.

Jyoti Juneja

A Wild Flower

She is a wild flower,
And they always loved roses.
She couldn't be a Rose,
No matter how hard she tried.
She couldn't make them happy.
She wasn't a Rose; and hence, she cried.
It wasn't her job to make others happy.
She was just meant to be herself.
For God gave her a different purpose,
That only wild flowers could do.
She was not meant to fit in.
Not meant for bouquets.
Not just an expression of love,
But a jewel of the crown,
That the mother Earth adores,
And carry it with pride.

A Little Bird

An adorable little bird,
Trapped in a golden cage,
Crushed at the hands of destiny.
She flaps, and flaps in rage.

Dreaming of the sky,
Ineffectual efforts go in vain.
Weeping out the heart
Feeling deep disdain.

Bars of gold ceased her freedom
Along with her desire to survive.
She looks up at the twinkling stars
As far as her dream, she deprived.

Confined little creature contemplates—
All Aves glorify the sky, not the cage.
Will this be my end?
Or my story got another page?

Death may embrace me anytime soon.
I would be a lover and elope.
Till my last breath I shall strive,
Nescient about my survival scope.

Cage neither preaches survival instincts,
Nor does it provide enough space to fly.
Naive knows not to endure the storms,
As their wings aren't well built for the sky.

Quest for Freedom

The world is a lake and I am sky.
Harder to recall, the harder I try.
The longer I gaze at the lake,
Confined I feel, despite my infinite stake.

A revolutionary heart,
Exploring directions in the dark.
So self-jeopardized,
One fine day, I realized—

Freedom is knowing thyself.
Not an answer locked in the bookshelf.
The deeper I dived to contemplate,
The quest culminated, and I could relate.

The cage is not the external bars,
But the conditioning of my mind.
Between my head and heart,
I continued to grind.

As the reign of silence overtook.
Everything became crystal clear.
For the mind as still as the lake,
The whispers of the soul—I could hear.

Monkey mind frolicking around,
Once it's tamed, you're no more bound.
The mind either confines or liberates,
Depending on its own tireless traits.

Her Moon

He was like the Moon,
She cherished from afar.
He kept on waning from her sky,
And enjoying the company of stars.

The stars never bothered her,
But she longed for her Moon.
Hoping he would comprehend,
And come back soon.

Enchanted

A fairytale,
A love story.
Rose tinted glasses—
It's all momentary.

Hit by the Cupid's bow and arrow—
Caged little Heart flies,
Roses begin to bloom,
Gazing at midnight skies.

Enchanted by the fragile velvety petals,
Its thorns are often overlooked.
One may get pricked in its proximity,
Stranded, spellbound, and still not unhooked.

For true love is a glorified gem,
That turns everything into gold.
A spirit that refrains from giving up
Can truly turn a coward into a bold.

Love is admiring the lord's creation.
Love knows not a reason to be.
A lover can be a fighter, but
It's not love if it doesn't set you free.

Misunderstood

What should I write
On a piece of paper?
Let the words imprint.
Let the pen cut a caper.

As nib jumps in the ink puddle,
A cord struck in my mind's dome.
My words often misunderstood,
My heart became a catacomb.

All these feelings underneath
Buried deep, deep inside.
The visage gleamed with a grin,
Carrying a dead heart alongside.

Whispers of the dead
Kept me awake at nights.
Molten magma expelled
Flowing through my eyes.

Like lifeless deserted island,
Into numbness I lie.
Meditating upon nothingness,
When I further could not cry.

An empty piece of paper
Remained empty for so long.
Until it rained, flowers bloomed,
Nature filled it with a song.

Let the pen cut a caper
To the symphony of heart.
Whether understood or not,
I have done my part!

A Burning Desire

A flame to fire.
A wish to a burning desire.
Interminable. Insatiable.
Getting it all—the world admires.

When fire gets out of hand.
Too late! Works no plan.
It can devour what comes its way.
Get the hell out! Don't be its prey.

Perishable perishes.
Not everything meant to stay.
Time is ticking.
All you can do is Pray.

Who Am I?

Who am I?
What I truly am.
Or what you see me to be.

Some see me as a confused character,
Some believe I possess an X-factor,
Some see me as an obnoxious introvert,
Some see me as a complex covert.

Some see me as touch-me-nots.
Some see me as an empty pot.
Some see me as a curious creature.
Some believe I dwell in literature.

Some see me as an honest soul.
Some see me as a wolf who howls.
Some see me as a know-it-all.
Some think—during my childhood—I had a fall.
(I actually did)

It is all in the mind.
The way you perceive, I become.
However, is it who I truly am?
Or is it just another identity I become?

What you think, you think.
What you see, you see.
But, don't let your mind shrink.
I'm not a leaf, but the whole tree.

Love Yourself

Walking under the scorching sun,
Devoid of love to satisfy the soul.
Feeling emptiness inside,
Seeking validation in life, you crawl.

Meant to walk, run and fly,
Choosing to be loved by others.
Triggered by their expectations,
Is this love, dear lovers?

Choosing to be someone you're not,
To witness your loved ones gleamed.
Don't you feel a void in your soul?
Is this what God deemed?

Postponing your soul purpose,
Not to offend them at present.
If that's the decision you make today,
Then later you'd surely repent.

How long would it take—
To love yourself?
How long would it take—
To be true to yourself?

Take a stand for what you believe.
Don't you wait for your soul to die.
Speak up your mind and stick to it.
Can't you hear your heart's cry?

Step out of the fences you mended.
Face your fears eye to eye.
For love asks for courage.
Don't you die before you die.

Loved ones would love the truer you.
Don't you sacrifice your purpose to be.
Spread your wings, flap and fly.
Because you are meant to be free.

Mind's Dark Alley

Down the darkest alley,
Shadows lurk around.
Can you hear it?
What's that sound?

Baffling barriers,
Rumbling noise.
Fight or flight.
You've the choice.

Heart beating,
Like a fire alarm.
Anxiety kicks in,
Hard to maintain calm.

Shivering sleek legs,
Quivering, clammy hands.
Facing the Monsters,
Mind's senseless rants.

Encircled with darkness,
Nothing you can see.
Foolish to believe the Mind,
How ludicrous could you be?

Surmount the situation,
Let the lamp of courage be lit.
Chuck "What-if" worst scenarios,
Be at peace, and mindful for a bit.

Monsters are in the mind.
Don't fight in vain.
Conserve your energy,
Don't take so much strain.

Visualize Best scenarios,
And the best you'd see.
Mind is just a projector,
Creating reality to be.

Pain

Carrying heart piercing pain,
And a quest in my eyes.
Each day, a struggle
With a smile that belies.

A wish of despaired heart
To elude from this pain.
Got no clouds in my sky.
How can I expect the rain?

Downhearted,
Helpless, hopeless, here I lie.
Why does my heart whisper—
"Give it one more try."

Pain unleashes the potential power,
That we never knew existed.
Burn like the Sun, to be the light.
Great Souls are the ones who persisted.

True Love

Love is a wild animal, living
In the dense jungle of the heart.
In disguise, he prevails.

When pure and devoted,
Stretching out to shine.
Purifying the kingdom,
To meet the divine.

Selfless as Lotus blooms,
And letting go all Glooms.
A Happy state of being,
And Heart begins to sing.

Detached from the flesh,
Seeking the divine in souls.
The Divine within,
Sees the Divine in all.

A wild animal,
That humbles the being.
Unlike the selfish swarm,
Collecting sweet, yet sting.

No sweet Love is enough,
The road to Love seems tough.
Not all battles are worth fighting,
As some are meant to walk away.

True love is a wild animal,
Not everyone can make it stay.

An Echo

On the hill top, I stand,
Staring at the hills abreast.
Yelling at them blaringly,
Only to see the mountains at rest.

An echo, I hear; loud and clear.
My voice came back hitting hills.
Reflecting, as a mirror for voice,
Mountains remain stubborn and still.

Watch out that what you say
Doesn't bring anyone to tears.
The words, I uttered, amplified
Before hitting back my ears.

Our actions create our reality.
Swinging between the world's duality.

I Love You

I love you.
I love you enough to let you go.
Seeds of love outgrown
That you never sow.

Can't blame you,
As you were never mine.
Love is like the Sun,
It will continue to shine.

For so long, it was hidden
Behind the clouds.
A resting bitch face,
And a heart full of doubts.

Sun can't stay hidden for long.
And so is Love.
The sky became clearer,
My heart flew like a dove.

People say — Love hurts.
However, I believe the contrary.
Expectations hurt. Distance hurts.
Love can never bind someone to marry.

So, Yes. I love you.
I love you enough to let you go.
Under the infinite sky of my heart,
A huge canopy of trees that you never sow.

My Home

Longing for a place I cannot find.
Ceaseless search blowing up my mind.
Trying to find my way back home,
A place of rest amidst a ruthless storm.

A home, not a structure of bricks and stones.
It could be someone with flesh and bones.
A place where I am unconditionally loved.
It could be someone my beloved.

Longing for a place that feels so safe,
Like an infant in a mother's embrace.
A place for which I'm longing for.
Safest on Earth where I belong.

The place I call home, nowhere to be found.
No matter how hard you try, or look around.
As it's not an ordinary place,
Where people rise even from disgrace.

The place I call home is divinely protected.
Where miracles are real, Expect the unexpected.
Each obstacle turns into an opportunity.
Faith, gratitude and God's grace create fortuity.

The place I call home is the Divine's refuge.
Stay strong even if the whole world accuse.
No one is above the creator of all.
He'll be your wings, whenever you'd fall.

God's Creation

Under a silver-lit night sky,
Staring at the stars, vividly I see.
Our galaxy, mere a leaf
Of a gigantic Galaxy tree.

Countless galaxy leaves
Bunch up to create the Universe.
Amongst all these thoughts
I found myself immersed.

This endless vast Universe
Created by God's desire.
Might leave you awestruck
The more you admire.

Magic fabricated in every atom,
For those who seek, would find.
We, one of God's greatest creations.
Why don't we practice being kind?

Mere a tiny little creature,
That will be crushed by Time,
With a limited period on Planet Earth
Contemplating a scientific paradigm.

The Scam

You say you care, and not a player.
My well-wisher, not my dream-slayer.
Pulling the strings to get your way.
Only trying to keep troubles at bay.

All you want for me is the best,
But every best has to pass the test.
My life is my journey.
God gave no one the power of attorney.

My soul purpose is solely mine.
Assigned by God, the true Divine.
The world thinks they know it all.
Ain't no support when they hear a call.

Leave me. Leave me be, as I am.
Insecurities ain't love, but a scam.

Now That I Am Gone

Now that I am gone,
You miss me now.
Wheel of fortune turned,
And I'm not around.

Here I am,
Writing my own success story.
With the Grace of God,
Every step towards golden glory.

Now that I'm gone,
You miss me now.
What's the point,
When I'm not around?

I was worthless back then.
Now, I mean the world to you.
What a sudden change?
You don't really love me, do you?

Now that I'm gone,
You miss me now.
What's the point,
When I'm not around?

I Forgive You

My heart knows not to hate.
With all my heart, I forgive you,
And leave you up to fate.

We all shall reap what we sow.
The seed of enmity, don't let it grow.
The weak avenge, strong let it go.

The Light Within

No one can dull your light,
When you shine from within.
Your radiance glows up glory.
The ecstasy you breathe in.

Stepping into the soul purpose,
Clearly now you see.
Everything was a distraction
From what you're meant to be.

You've always been the Sun,
Cloaked behind the clouds of doubts.
Unconscious of your gifts,
And lost in the whereabouts.

All it took was the courage,
To be who you truly are.
So what if you burn within?
You're the galaxy's brightest star.

The Glory of God gleams within.
For you're merely a creation of his.
Believe in yourself and cherish—
His blessings, abundance and bliss.

Choose Yourself

The divinity you seek in others
Dwells within you as well.
When would you realize it?
Wake up if it rings a bell.

Wake up before it's too late.
Life is short, and dreams can't wait.
Prioritize yourself, take your stand.
Don't wait for any helping hand.

Leave! Leave your comfort zone.
Accept and move towards the unknown.
Let your soul show you the way.
Don't let distractions get you swayed.

Not making a choice is also a choice.
Let your success shush all the noise.
You can't make everybody happy.
If the world is a sad song, then be a peppy.

Choose your happiness above everyone else.
The world would cheer you—it's a pretense.
From coal to diamond—a long story.
Without persisting pressure, there's no glory.

www.ingramcontent.com/pod-product-compliance
Lightning Source LLC
LaVergne TN
LVHW010932200726
843509LV00013B/2181